NSCV

CV ~~9/05~~	CX	CY ~~06/07~~	NA	NB
NL	NM	PL	PO	WB
WL	WM	WN	WO ~~3/06~~	WS ~~5/08~~

Please return/renew this item by the last date shown.

North
Somerset
COUNCIL

SCATTERING EVA

SCATTERING EVA

James Sheard

CAPE POETRY

Published by Jonathan Cape 2005

2 4 6 8 10 9 7 5 3 1

Copyright © James Sheard 2005

James Sheard has asserted his right under the Copyright, Designs
and Patents Act 1988 to be identified as the author of this work

First published in Great Britain in 2005 by
Jonathan Cape
Random House, 20 Vauxhall Bridge Road, London SW1V 2SA

Random House Australia (Pty) Limited
20 Alfred Street, Milsons Point, Sydney,
New South Wales 2061, Australia

Random House New Zealand Limited
18 Poland Road, Glenfield,
Auckland 10, New Zealand

Random House South Africa (Pty) Limited
Endulini, 5A Jubilee Road, Parktown 2193, South Africa

The Random House Group Limited Reg. No. 954009
www.randomhouse.co.uk

A CIP catalogue record for this book is
available from the British Library

ISBN 0-224-07584-5

Papers used by Random House are natural,
recyclable products made from wood grown in sustainable forests;
the manufacturing processes conform to the environmental
regulations of the country of origin

Typeset by Palimpsest Book Production Limited, Polmont, Stirlingshire
Printed and bound in Great Britain by Biddles Ltd, King's Lynn, Norfolk

for Helen

CONTENTS

ACKNOWLEDGEMENTS

Acknowledgements are due to the following publications:

London Review of Books,
Avocado, Matter, Proof

A number of these poems were collected in the pamphlet
Hotel Mastbosch (Mews Press, 2003) and in *Ten Hallam Poets*
(Mews Press, 2005)

AT KONSTANZ

Each time a villa fronts a lake,
let there be white wood shutters.
Let curved ironwork hang
with geranium and vine.
Let the maples make a *paseo*.

In the lock of land and heat,
my thoughts drone slow as Zeppelins.

No Hesse, I. No Dix, no Hus,
no Magister Hieronymus.
For one brief hour at each last light,
the mountains rise − distant, pale.

Doch, unscaled.

HOTEL MASTBOSCH

Old money smells of civet, folds in
and whispers *scurf* and *scrofula*.
Its women oil pearls at nutmeg throats,
sure-fingered as a Chinese tallyman
clicking behind a carved Sumatran screen.

There are flickers of acknowledgement,
eyes with the tilt and swivel of loose rivets,
noses which lift and flare
above whole vanished islands of spice.

And then the sounds of shunting-yards,
chased silver bracelets clanking down
on varnished tables, the huffy dismissals
of steam trains settling.

      The evening thickens
to a brown frottage of old wallpaper,
sticky with molasses, pressed tobacco,
the renderings of shelled insects.

Above it all,
the slap of leather and brass:
a trundle turning fans as if in Java,
cooling old fevers
and the orange of their bones.

DÉCLASSÉ

With a kicking-over of cauldrons
the valleys skew and clatter –
Sheffield's spiking light.

On a dark handle of the lifted hills
we click and shift – sore teeth
in a grey gumline of parkland,

watching stairwells invert,
piss-streaks heard roofwards,
the clatter and glitter of needles.

The chi-chi quarters pulse wet
and shudder with Chinese collections.
Fat florets of *kir*. A sudden *curaçao*.
The sticky yellows of dessert wines.

We hold the hooks and barbs
of keymetal. Coins can jut usefully
between knuckles. Bottles lie everywhere.

We trek back with empty hands
thinking of impromptu weaponry.

STUDYING SANTIAGO

At Seu Vella,
our climb is watched
by lidded towers
smudged with Islam.

Among the slablike light
and the Calibanate grafts
of fortress architecture
there's a cloister –
cool and helpless,
a handful of powder snow
feathering away.

So I talk of the crumblings
of kingdoms and caliphates –

– *of kindness*, you say,
studying Santiago,
and tell me of kissing
my poisoned hem, of digging
knuckledeep in my roots
and finding stone.

Then turning against the light,
you give me his names:
Pilgrim. Slayer.

HEADING FOR PORT BOU, 1939

The refugees stood aside, while the canvasses of Velázquez, Goya, Titian, Rubens passed. Azaña . . . remarked to Negrín that all notions of monarchy and republic were not worth a single Velázquez. Negrín agreed. Neither, of course, believed it.

Hugh Thomas, *The Spanish Civil War*

Towards Figueras, late winter deadened
the dry scents of low scrub and lavender;
trucks dragged axles like broken hindquarters,
taking agonies and annunciations into exile.

Behind us, Barcelona had broken open
like an egg, leaking poisons and rumour,
sinuous and Gaudí-curved, the pendulous tongues
and blank-eyed duty of late killings.

The squabbling rump of the Cortes met
in dungeons, farmhouses, spread the flag
on rough tables, hurled ultimata behind them,
like the farting of our ill-fed mules. We thought

of the Caudillo, nodding in his darkened room,
his carved Crusader's head long turned to Baphomet.

THE LOST TESTIMONY OF
R. CATESBY

The gentler tortours are to be first usid unto him, et sic per gradus ad ima tenditur

James I to Fawkes' interrogators

The night had that distant glitter of marcasite.
We rode northwest,
steaming off our chain of horses.

I fumbled largesse at the waystations;
struck fresh reins from the nervous hands of ostlers.
It seemed the turf peeled back,
and the bones of recusant England
tore loose beneath us.

We had left women to watch
the hurdles and quartering-tables;
ravel up the tawdry miracles of the scaffoldside.
Lips might twitch in a held-up head;
blood shape a face on a cornhusk.

They slammed the fact of Reformation shut
on Guido's hands. Those thick fingers
cut tapers, drew maps, bent barrelhoops
an extra inch. He told me once

we had lived too long
as spiders in the curtains.

Now I think of his strength
decaying like dead powder;
of dim ships slipping back into Biscay fog,
carrying their sour cargo
of questions
and instruments.

THE NAMES OF TOWNS

Here we pass the closed cold churches,
their spaces hung between us.

And there the homes of churning mills,
the scored stone weights of love.

We make there-there mouths of consolation,
or gestured, distant kisses.

We eat. We make our sounds
of contempt, or of sorrow.

We pass towns, cross borders,
occupy one another somehow.

CALLS TO PRAYER

When you call me
to break words with you,
as if we could break them like bread,

I hear your clarities, the call of muezzins,
slim white towers in the clean morning.

But what prayers I have are for you
and not for you to share.

What words I have to break
are those which long since laid
these sad flat beaches,

and hollowed out these empty stages.

TENDER

Lord, how that April mugged us,
its two fists full of fresh wet things,
and me grabby, and you gripping wrought iron
topped with malformed fleurs-de-lys.

That English of yours – careful, silvery –
you let a little history drop.
It made you almost unfuckably
tender. But not quite. Not then.

Bright L, vague diphthong, an extra breath.
Läh- Läh- Lähde, meaning fountain,
or spring, or source – or some such thing, loosed
unstuttering from a firm, clean earth.

These nights, I wedge my gut to the mattress side.
Snores slide like pinecones between my teeth.

HIGH TIDE, BOSHAM

I

When a high tide pushes up
to Bosham's walls in shuffled rows,
mortar shifts.

The gulls call time
on feeding. Locals hop nimble
over high lintels,
button up tatty waders,
let Bosham settle
tidily.

Crowns of lost kings
bump along rim-marked rocks.
Poor Cnut sat up
to ageing kneecaps here,
intent on quashing
the oily claims of courtiers.

What cruelty legends do!
A miracle his noble name's
not worse mis-spelled.

II

A slender tide thins your ashes
in evening water. Father-ashes,
slow and stately. Father: ashes.

The channel holds us for a moment –
the slack tide's heart-flutter.

Gulls clatter up from the prow.

Cnut's ghost is here somewhere,
still grumbling.
Grant us, King, this miracle:
A turning-back
of this minute's turning,
this slackened heartbeat.

CARGO CULT

In an imperfect incense
of soil and old candles
the kept objects sit
on split grey shelving –
dull cones of lead, broken tools,
bits of strange bracketry.

For a while I fake
the slimfingered expertise
of a collector turning porcelain,
before letting my square hands
hang and rust.

Tumbled here like cargo
from the metal perfection
of a distant father, pinning me
between fool and acolyte,

between turning and waiting
a quiet unscowling moment longer
for him to return

and tell me what these things were
and why it was they mattered.

THE BUOY YARDS

Some mornings can be this,
a sliding scale.
Piped notes or value, I'm undecided.

Here to sing descant, I'm numb
at the rushing train window,
big-boned from short sleep.

It's pure lowland, Dutch,
still fields, a broken fence,
still horses in the still morning.

We pass buoy yards. Garish, riveted
the shock of so many impossibly together –

Such lolling, monstrous *mots-justes*! Primed
with their one note, one sound –
the one I lack, the one that gives sense

to the where, the why, the being
amidst my gentle, if empty, horizons.

SALTAIRE

The chimneybases are slabbed and massive
in the valley of a singular King.
Here Titus squared his wealth, cubed it,
raised goldmean elevations:
Window, detail and pediment
moving fullsquare and endless,
an autistic penwork seeming set to shrink the hills.

He named streets for his family,
planted foremen's houses like mileforts
among the low tenements. Gumption, betterment –
the adults learnt strictures on hygiene,
saw drink banished from the precincts
while children skittered past stone lions
and snaked to their separate entrances.

*

My grandfather spoke schoolmasterly,
his careful enunciations strewn
with nowts and nobbuts.
I minded missen and thought on –
we never owned mills nor worked them,
but fed them with wool the colour of stale butter
from scraggy blackfaces raised west of Ilkley.

But Titus used alpaca,
bale after bale bought on thumbrubs
on a Liverpool wharf. In Ravensthorpe and Dewsbury
rose an industry of remnants,
shredding woollens for mungo,
worsteds for shoddy,
the tough fibrous cloths of Low Calder voices.

★

Carding, Combing, Secondary Dyeing –
the flagged and vaulted spaces unthrummed
and declattered. Some chatter, true,
at the lilies flown in by Hockney,
and murmurs at his hung boys on pale tiled floors –
the utter evenness of Californian light untroubled
by rain dragging reluctant feet over Baildon
to starken the glassine cobbling.

CAFE VERDI

We feel rough and pitted as promenade rails,
our talk a slapdash glosswork
between the slack voltage of the sea
and our backboard of facts and old houses.

Our planes and angles are set awry,
a hasty laying of seafront flagstones
or the cafe rising in a drunken hedron
of glass and grey weathering.

We make fingertip searches
through the offsquare weave of cheap napkins,
consider *ciabatta and cheddar*
as the waiter's Welsh-Italian makes arcs and tangents,
the stumbles of an acrobat.

I have new blueprints to unfold.
A tracery of new alignments to knucklelock
above the tabletop. Hands to circle intersections
of clarity and need.

But she traces a more faded line.
Brief lives of the rockpool creatures.
The bright-eyeing of market treats.
Squabbling daytrips to misjudged threepoints
in the tight inland lanes.

So as Verdi assembles his playhouse
from primaries and angled tubing
I tell her of the climbing frame
which, as children, we would dress
with bolts of threaded straw.
Then crawl in
and call it home.

FOUR MIRRORS

He bought four mirrors
from a sale of kitsch fitments –
silvered plastic tricked up
for a warping of bodies and light.

It was wrong to hang them foursquare
down the dead cream walls of renting,
placed to catch the phone
and his fakir stillness.

Because he bulged; skinned over
with the pierced stone eye of a lizard;
and bent into strychnine loops
of mixed fruits and kaleidoscoping.

Sometimes he rippled like a washboard,
and found ribs, a whole history
of sidesteps and shifting;

or raised a thickwalled cup
which flared out like a medium
spewing cheesecloth, in that moment
before the sceptics rise
and pounce.

THE WINTER SINGLES

Winter has an obscure way of hoping,
a palsied face grown frozen
and pressed to the window.

It makes words miraculously unformed,
speech a scarce creation,
crammed and cooling in the throat.

And although it calls for cello music,
these forks of cloud,
these cyclones of moonlight,

we hear only voices through the wall:
Almost-known, the dim open vowels of snow.

UCCELLO'S DRAGON

Paolo's a master of mosaics,
shuffling purblind on bound knees.

He scrats for tiles in the rough-worked box,
hears his wife's tongue jump back
from the ridge of her teeth, that click
she knuckles from the fantail latch.

From the market, she fetches
smoked junipers to embitter him,
capers from the walls of looted stone
to keep him sour – Paolo frets

about the tack and give of mortar,
how to curl sketched edges
of map and theory into held objects.
He dreams of bright hedra.

One day he will triangulate her
into allegory, turn her ground
to coiled ash, make dentals
of her bland face and ambivalence.

Or glance up – the lance already sunk
and splintering in his hapless eye.

J.V. PROSPERO

Night sinks its wells among the trees, sketches
wolves' heads in the underhangs. Land and water
heave a while, then lie in great blocks over Winter.

Some comrades have not yet learnt to wait:
one bumps bloated along the thickening river;
another blackens his bones in a hut fire. Warm

at last, eh? But the living things, too, trail steely
vapours to empty traps, to battered settlements,
to a little sense of elsewhere. As for me,

twelve birds hang like gloves on the beam-hooks.
I pad gently through these years in felt boots.
Send news. Send books. I'll not burn 'em.

ULRIKE IN STAMMHEIM

Fucking and shooting, it's the same thing.

Andreas Baader

Roth-Händles were always rough on my Schili throat.
I looted Mao for the tracts, moved among the people
like a fish through silt – fumbling ordnance
and stuttering on the setting of watches. Still,

they will tie white sheets around the bars
to make a cross. The guards will grow surly,
wielding doors that muffle shut like the stuffing
of mouths with cloth – *Not one word. Not one.*

Fucking's not Praxis. That's more creak and flake,
another dud weld that hyphenates his name to mine.
I coil in on the eel-loop of rifling, grow heavy with oils,
and dull to the grey bloom of fingers pressed to metal.

And nothing haunts like the dumb fact of a thing: My
    children
with strangers; lawyers springing from my broken teeth.

Stammheim: prison in which members of RAF (Baader-Meinhof) were held
Roth-Händles: a brand of strong, filterless cigarettes; a 'worker's smoke'
Schili: a German elision of 'chic' and 'left'; faux-radical

FORTIES

Forget for now the idiot sea
beyond the glass,
its angry, melting-bar-iron glares,
its idiot anger,
our idiot selves.

Of what we might feign,
we choose sleep
or remembrance –
our faces setting slowly
into empty angers.
Beyond us,
low sun stains the seawindow glass
and the colours of an African mask
stare angrily in.

And watch my sleeping anger.
Humbly, I make my quiet plans
for fury – and draw you in.
Behind us, the mile-wide wake
of my cunning: So simple,
from the horizon to here;
so hugely white,
so slowly feverish.

The earth's curve snaps horizons
into endless lengths
of equal size:
We touch to its order
the hot coals of our waiting,
or give ourselves
to all these blind upheavals:
Childlike,

sacrificial,
the salt in our silent mouths.

At the time we left,
a tug wreck at the tide edge
lifted a tired head,
then let it drop.
Had the moon sunk
her fat fingers a little deeper,
we might all yet heave clear
of the sea's fallen girders.

THE NO-SAYER

Stars shiver
on the edge of elimination,
these nightwater histories
of ivory and architecture.

Cold bell, the cold loops
of the counted blessings –

the ward's flowerbruised brightness,
the slow blossoms
of hurt.

★

November, things bloom –
fireballs
from small villages,

blood
on rough cloth,

the bruises
his fingers
forced from you.

Things bloom
in the November poem.

★

We cast bronzes from rage,
surfaces
moving with illogical shadow.

Brief clutters of birdsong.

Winched upwards from our cooling,
nothing stirs –

locked musclehollows
locked shawlings-in of hair.

★

You move lonewards, tilt nowards,
gesture, as if tired,
towards some word or other.

My dissidence,
a hunching-along
in these slicings of North and angles.

And when even the floodriver
momentarily dissents,
its flat tablings of stillness –

there's no space,
no words
from the no-sayer.

WRITING HISTORY

You looked at me,
looked away. The mouth
spoke its way to eye,
I heard:

Paul Celan, *Zurich, The Stork Inn*

Days now, weeks, of swinging lead
against gable-ends and tinted walls
in salmons, limes, eggshell blues,
those pale yolks that take a mural well.

Old towns laid with herringbone
drag our feet onwards, back. To
one more square, one more cup,
one more plaque to Goethe's roaming.

At The Stork, we don't make the terrace.
My shoes, perhaps; your scruffy coat.
So we'll be no Paul and Nelly swirling cream
above dark talk of death and God.

Celan was master of what the eye
would say. He'd see mine swing
to where the Minster scatters scraps
of red and gold in the green Limmat.

But nothing speaks. Nothing says
how last night's cries —
animal-far, around me —
could be hers.
That one late frost

might catch the past-dawn grass
*that now – **now** – it will not melt.*
That we pray for nothing.
That life's taste, lifelong,
is unsanctified ashes,
uncircled with fear.
That we can die.
That we cannot die
insignificantly.

I look to you, then look away
to gable ends and tinted walls
in salmons, limes, eggshell blues,
pale yolks that take a mural well.

Scattering Eva

PROLOGUE

Ich weiss dass die Welt gross und schlecht ist,
hart und ungerecht ist.[1]

Sabrina Setlur, *Du Liebst Mich Nicht*

It's a coastlit afternoon,
the leaded windows briefly holy,
and Eva – briefly –
has no elegies to sing.

Nothing of the land that broke her feet.
Burnt carpentries. Broken sleepers.
Canals with their undertows of rust.
Nothing, this time, of that fist
unclenching in the rubble of Altona.

She says the earth caught her sidestep.
She straddles the German Bight.
Eva, our Colossus.

⋆

I tell Eva we are cracked bells,
heard over water,
swinging hard
against swallowed harmonics.

And I tell her how no word is whole,

uprooted from our thesauri,
from those scrapyards of locked metal.

Na, Schatz[2], says Eva, *No flower is plucked
without the ground shaking.*

          ★

And beneath her voice,
some touchstone.
Beneath its bluntness,
more.

Beneath winter,
the bones of the earth
might bend a little.

And so might image be broken
into thought; thought be broken
into syntax.

          ★

Sometimes the sea is all centres,
heaving up its sledgehammers to my heart.

And sometimes I think of an ocean,
pouring back from all coasts,
into itself.

[2] sweetheart, darling

Of something fallen,
closed-in,
crystal.

Of how light might cut it through,
infinite and unescaping.

Tchaa. One night under the bombs
would drown you.

★

Bunker people,
they were made of dust.

Soup-greens sprouted unpulled
among the shovelled houses.

The wife of a silenced man,
mother of dead sons,
offered me the peel
from a piece of fruit.

It dogs me, Schatz,
like a fact, like a limb.
But not a shadow. For
no shadow could narrow
quite as mine has
in your sun.

★

The moon in the late morning sky
cannot fool me:
it's simply distant,
grieving.

I watch its thin beacon,
draw in the sea's dead smell
before it slips back and leaves me – exile
without movement.

Naja, and so on.

But soon, Schatz. Float down the Elbe
one day soon, Schatz.
Tell them Eva's coming home.

★

You're a moral man. Yes,
my pinched and wintry -Isms
now lock me under,
now join the insane clatter of the thaw.

And if nature awaits,
she offers no evidence – *Ja,*
the carnage of late winter.

★

When there were still Sundays
and Fathers, we marched
around the Alster, father leading.

Snow lay in bulbs
around the dark benches.
The white earth bled snowdrops.
Our breath seemed printed
on the river's slow winter.

I sat quiet and small at Oelke's Cafe
among stiff linen and heavy silver.
I darkened my mouth with cocoa and cake.
I sat quiet and small
and I let nothing fall

and I was

good

★

Eva, lion,
shaking that dyed and misjudged mane
from the mantlepiece.

Eva, lollhead, sipping feebly
at thin clarity – another day
from the held cup.

★

On the soft back of Fairlight,
Eva's senses return to rubble.

The iron loops of land and time
feed into one another
and the ground beneath her.

See, Eva, how the water tolerates
the blind scrabbling of the light!
Hear how the earth hums with geodesy!

Du . . . breathes Eva. And yes,
my every word
is the last drop of blue
on a black match-head.

EVA'S HOMECOMING

Neuer Wall (ehm. Dreckwall)[3]

(Exhibit Label, Museum of Hamburg History)

When I moored up
against the hulk of Hamburg,
gulls rose
on the cries of shiphands.

Bismarck bowed his head.

Overnight, the wind
had fought the light a little.
Thin cloud had made a petal of the moon,
laid scales on the sea's grey hide.

It failed to rise. It failed
to shake me loose.

Last night, a woman walked
in the night ship's diesel hum,
her cotton shift trailing soiled
over dusty feet. The nub
of each outer toe lifted
to sail above the decks.

I saw her then in Baltic furs,
bristling with vanillas.

I saw her, too, as Eva,
now twenty years dead.

[3] New Dyke (formerly Crap Dyke)

37

★

I carry Eva's ashes –

Poor Eva's ashes.
Eva's muttering, restless ashes.
Eva's fucking ashes.
Those fucking ashes of Eva's –

I carry Eva's ashes
to the landing-bridges.

What's treulos, *Schatz?*
Faithless? Feckless?
Untrue? *Ja,*
all those.

★

Hamburg hunkers over the Elbe
like a woman pissing in a stream.

Heh.

★

I see you darning
the things I would discard.

I see you on the night verandah,
darning the things I would discard.

Your eyes cast downwards.
Your hair tied up.
Your hands old,
but curved like silver,
quick as seedlings,
darning the things
I would discard.

My skin filling.
The fountain in your name.
And my throat, tongue, jaw
all locked.

Na gut.
Just take the yellow line, Schatz.
The one like that.
Like that streak
that striped your back.

*

They wore nailed boots,
stomped in from the North-West
on tubes of light.

*

St Pauli. Here, fire streamed westward
towards the tenements.

Now shapes move against the light,
duck in doorways.
The cocksure and cock-sore,
grabbing what they can carry.

★

Here's Sternschanze, the meat quarter.
Tuesday's blood day. The smell
hangs like lead curtains.

Na, what now, Schatz?
The chapped face and snarls
of the woman serving Wurst?

Those things you think.
That, once torn, we cannot heal.
That we cannot answer for what is done.

That my slackened hand
would never dip between my legs
at thoughts of you
and not-you.

She should swing her paw
and cuff you, Schatz.
Someone should
now I am gone.

*

Once,
to feel what warmed her,
I watched a woman move
among old boxes and light.

Some blonded,
some dull-honeyed,
but all hunched and darkening
under high ceilings.

I was there to feel wary, to watch how –
having leached out the dark businesses
of growth, joy, a reaching-out –
they greedily gathered light to themselves.

And I was there to feel what should warn me –
how wood –
how we –
can be crafted to this deceit:

Our locks, slots and dovetails
clicking neatly shut
on our emptinesses,
our dark holdings of space,

our as-if-content closures.

TRADING HISTORY

Und kaum war er in der Partei[4]
Max Frisch, *Biedermann und die Brandstifter*

Going down,
the withanotherdaygorged sun.

I read *Eine von Diesen*[5]
beneath a crematorium clock.

Well, that's a certainty.
A wire garotte
beneath hard cellar lights.

Going about my purpose.
Wondering why I hear nothing.

★

That language – your language –
and my age, now. The body
cannot shake those toxins.
They lodge in the liver, the lung.

But what lingers in the spine, Schatz?
I kicked at night. You slithered
through my day.

[4] And he was hardly in the Party at all
[5] One of These

★

Eva, daughter of a bourgeois house.
High ceilings behind pastelled Jugendstil.
Furniture rising like black cliffs.

A little man, he was, Schatz.
Common, to use the word.
Fit to doff a cap, to touch
a lank forelock. A little man
fit to take your luggage
to the train-step.

But he trotted, did he not,
through your old corridors,

sniffing at aniseed and schmalz,
ear cocked to a marzipan waltz,
to a boarhunter's shout
among the dripping trees.

Baroque, he was —
blackening your secret churches
with skulls and scrollwork.

★

Also, Ev'chen, echt kein wort?
kein *wussten-nicht* für deinen Schatz?[6]

---

[6] So, little-Eva, really no word? / No *didn't know* for your 'Schatz'?

A little heap of silence glitters
around a black pearl.

★

So break me the bells and walls
of the dolorous North.

Nail Luther to St Peter's door.

Let the squat, stubby cocks
of Bismarck's towers sink
beneath smothering treelines.

★

So you wore nailed boots,
stomped in from the North-West
on tubes of light.

Schatz, we lived
among the torn sides of a crucible,
seething beneath a month of lead.

At the Zoo sidings, the animals boiled
in their crates. Boy Helmie
carried his dead brother
to the watching suburbs
in a rag papoose.

Think,
if you will,
of the weight.

And listen, Schatz, listen.
For the thump that would suck air
from our concrete vaults,
and make black Lavinias
of us all.

★

Palm Sunday, Lübeck. Christ has taken
Jerusalem, the burghers settle at oak tables.
Europe capers through its Todestanz.

This night, a little Gehenna will be tipped,
a little late, down the white throats
of Petri, Maria, Michel. The bells will fall

to lie soft-buckled in pits of shattered tiles.
Here's the soot-stained Christ of the Limbless,
of the Torso, and the Helpless Hand. Here's Mary,

clutching a stone book, the clasps blown off.
Whatever word it holds will never drift
from these gutted roofs.

★

The centre never gutters, Schatz.
We are mere kindling to history.

Our clothes, our hair, our skin, too –
plucked and flashed-off like cobwebs.

Pitch and colour shrieking inwards
at the speed of a hurricane,
tumbling the lucky into craters
with a little water from a broken pipe.

Sucking fat from the mothers.

Children lay like smoked eels
on the doorsteps.

*

In the breakfast-room,
the ladies are complaining of little sleep.

The men who melted in the East –
Ach, Papi –
watch from mantlepieces.
Broad shoulders. Level gazes.

They jostle there like gables
in a town of bankrupt merchants.

*

Pastor Bärbel, between organ phrases,
modulates Iraq. She drips a little Goethe,
Freud, the marginalia of a mediaevalist:

'Let there be no stone for the German dead.
No carved names for a finger to trace.
Let the dead lie together in our far homeland.
A thing which blooms can never end.'

Naja. *Naja.*

SELFSPEECH

Wir
wissen nicht, weisst du,
wir
wissen ja nicht,
was
gilt.[7]

Paul Celan, *Zürich, zum Storchen*

It's a language of utterances,
of end-stops. You wait

for all that's held-back,
dragged and stacked.

It's turn.
Then silence.
Then turn-again.

The silence might be a scrap
of perfumed cloth,
held to the nose –

Eva, in her faded, little-girl best
among the streaked corpses.

★

---

[7] We / don't know, you know / we / just don't know / what / counts.

To measure a circle, Schatz,
start nowhere.

Walk it round.
Stand centrally.

Let the landscape fall –
useless, uninformed –
away.

★

Ready to listen, Schatz?
Listen? As judge, perhaps.

I will be all snowlight,
all cold source,
as I watch your shadows
confess themselves.

I will listen
as the numb morning once listened –
songless, thawless –
to my footstep on buckled grass.

I will listen like crystal,
and sing faintly
to the warm corrupted wines
of your dark and struggling heart.

★

Sprache, mein Ersticken.
Speech, my suffocation.

Wörter, meine Totengräber, Wörter:
Words, my gravediggers, words:
wie mütig, wie tot –
brave, dead –

Ich stand –
I stood –
die gepeitschten weissen Wände des Leuchtturms
the lashed white walls of the lighthouse.
Möwen getragen von meinem Schrei –
Gulls sat back on my cry.

★

I was born to the Colonies.
Blond little-Peter to the Greek widows,
spoilt roundeye to the Amah.

Between the rains,
sack-rice was spread on the flatstone.
Weevils streamed away
like sin.

All your mothers, Schatz.
We shine a strange light.

★

I remember waking
to our tactful, English occupation
of Evaland.

A narrow valley cupped me
as if in Dürer's praying hands –
or the meat
in a half-open mussel.

The dark stub
of a Bismarck tower
poked above the treeline.

Taktvoll, Takt, taktieren[8] –

the slippery English
tipping doubt into our wells.

*

And what happens when there is ease, Schatz,
a fluid between your heart and creation?

Then the world ceases.
The air is iron, the sky
hooded, the sea
sheet-metal, and all
unyielding.

Frozen for my moment
and brittle with its passing.

[8] tactful, rhythm, 'strategise'

★

We come in on one heartbeat,
and cease on another.

And mistime the rhythm
which chains the two.

And if we surge on,
the world swelling in us,
what other world sets itself
against us?

★

I stood in a sick light
in the shattered oldtown.

I turned myself
to the cooling world,
to the pincers meeting.

It's been a slow century, Schatz,
a leaking-away of the light,

a regime,
tired and dimming.

★

Words. Words
and a cold-chisel.

I would cast you
among iron leaves
in grey woods
in a grainy light.

Fodder for a slow beast.

                   ★

So let some stillness settle in me.
Let my hair hang heavy
in a heavy frost.

I spiralled to you
with some sense of love,
some heartbeat.

As prey, as hunter,
as either,
we watch the shut-down skyline
as if for justice.

DUET

1. Do you pity women?
2. Why/Why not?

Max Frisch, Self-Questionnaire in *Diaries 1966–71*

I always knew how to triangulate
my women –

Täter, Opfer, Retter[9].

I placed you upon the point
of that witch's straddle.

★

Oils, muscle, bits
of speech. They stir
no shadow

in the metal hollow of my cheek.

★

Once,
and behind you,
thin smoke lazed up
from a late Summer hillside of trees.

---

[9] Perpetrator, Victim, Rescuer

It made the light briefly graphic,
touched it with forever,
missing us.

★

Forever, Schatz.
That's a crystal so rare
that its forming meets
with its evaporation.

A fluid within us,
beyond us,
forever.

★

We're all happiest
in dishonesty, in denying
that we are fine china
or two faces in silhouette.

I was somewhere, something
among our muddy words.

You were something –
fragmentary but not frail –

an image on bright porcelain,

unearthed.

★

That gaze! A hostile sun
on a failing crop.

I gather in my hair,
my skirts,
my corn.

★

Sometimes you would weave me
in crossing spotlight.
I would crawl in webbing,
in uptorn shrubs.

Later, I'd watch your ribs
rise and fall – sandbars
in a sloping tide.

The room darkening.

★

Now that was something
to be gathered in. Silked-

in, Schatz,
like the finest thread.

Something to send your blood
billowing through you.

★

We are stone, Schatz –
stone marred by clumsy sculpting.

Stone from which nothing
has quite been freed.

★

Or we fall,
as if between mirrors.

Reflections flower out
along each axis. Horizons
curl in on one another.

At some distance, that row
of bound bodies,
tapered and flaming.

We light the processionals
of some bored tyrant.

★

And then you shadow
the window.
Touch me.
Delicate star.
Scent.

We watch the impacting air
lay ice on the outer-decks,
welding sky to metal,
fear to sea,
the earth to elsewhere.

And I am traceless, extant,
so much myself, here –

cancelling history,
my eyes fixed strangely godwards.

In this woman's animal smell,
in this heaven of contempt.
In paralysis. In ascension.

EPILOGUE

The picture of the Meistersingers presented by Wagner is highly romanticised; except to the specialist, the literature of 'Meistergesang' is of an appalling dullness.

Leonard Forster, *German Verse*

I scatter Eva

Think of yourself as broken,
crossing some scrubby border,

171.
Lord of fragments, Lord of burns
Lord of hope and blind eye turned
Lord of ordnance, Lord of kills
Lord of little, yet Lord still.

at the Elbe's rattling edges

defecting from these borrowed homelands
of image and register.

Lord in twilight, Lord at bay,
Lord who looks the other way,
Lord of hiltless rusted sword
Lord dismantled, yet still Lord.

unmodified

Or think of yourself alone,
the light gone,

Let nations hide their borders,
Let our fat world hide its girth,
Let oceans still their waves
And their flatterings of lace.

in a Hamburg twilight

creating yourself whole
from each careful mouthful
of careful language.

Let halting, tuneless voices
Lift our hymns above the earth
And sigh through Eva's ashes
Of our godlessness, and grace.

in a Hamburg rain

Think of each responsible word!

250.
All the scattered, Lord,
the broken and the lost,

I lift my eyes

Like stories told
at a long-closed border crossing.

slumped in endless deserts
in blue and aching frosts,

to a Hamburg sky

> *Words. Then*
> *moments of light in the iris.*

>> All those you scatter, Lord
>> the un-cursed and de-blessed,

and roll them, *Herr,*

> *Then words.*

>> Let them rest
>> Let them rest

as Eva might.

>> Let them rest.